AF598779

The LENTEN ADVENTURES with FATHER NATE

By Mia Toschi & Madalyn Allender Illustrated by Amanda Jozaitis

CATHOLIC.
PASTORAL.
TRUSTED.

Published by Liguori Publications, Liguori, Missouri 63057

Liguori Publications, a nonprofit corporation, is an apostolate of the Redemptorists (Redemptorists.com).

Phone: 800-325-9521 Web: Liguori.org

The Lenten Adventures With Father Nate,
Mia Toschi and Madalyn Allender

ISBN 978-0-7648-2903-1
E-ISBN: 978-0-7648-7283-9

Cover design: Amanda Jozaitis

Printed in the United States of America
29 28 27 26 25 / 5 4 3 2 1
Second Edition

This book was created to teach children about the Catholic faith and the Lenten season and to help form children as young disciples. The book also introduces children to saints celebrated in Lent and provides suggested activities and prayers for children and families.

Free educational resources are available online at **thecatholicadventures.org**

Father Nate is a Catholic parish priest in Indiana.

Father Nate is a Catholic priest who lives in a beautiful town with a lot of lakes. He likes to do many things, including exercising, playing instruments, and cooking healthy foods. He always finds God's gifts that are everywhere.

When he plays his tuba, he learns new music. When he cooks healthy foods from other countries, he learns about different cultures. When he kayaks, he gets good exercise.

His friends call him an adventurer because he likes to try new things.

Let's go on an adventure with Father Nate through the 40 days of Lent.

Easter
Sunday
Holy Saturday
40
Good
Friday
39
38
Holy
Thursday
37
36
35
Palm
Sunday
34
33
32
31
30
29
5th
Sunday
28
27
26
25
24
23
4th
Sunday
22
21
20
19
18

Father Nate begins each morning by saying his prayers. One of his favorite prayers is the **Glory Be.**

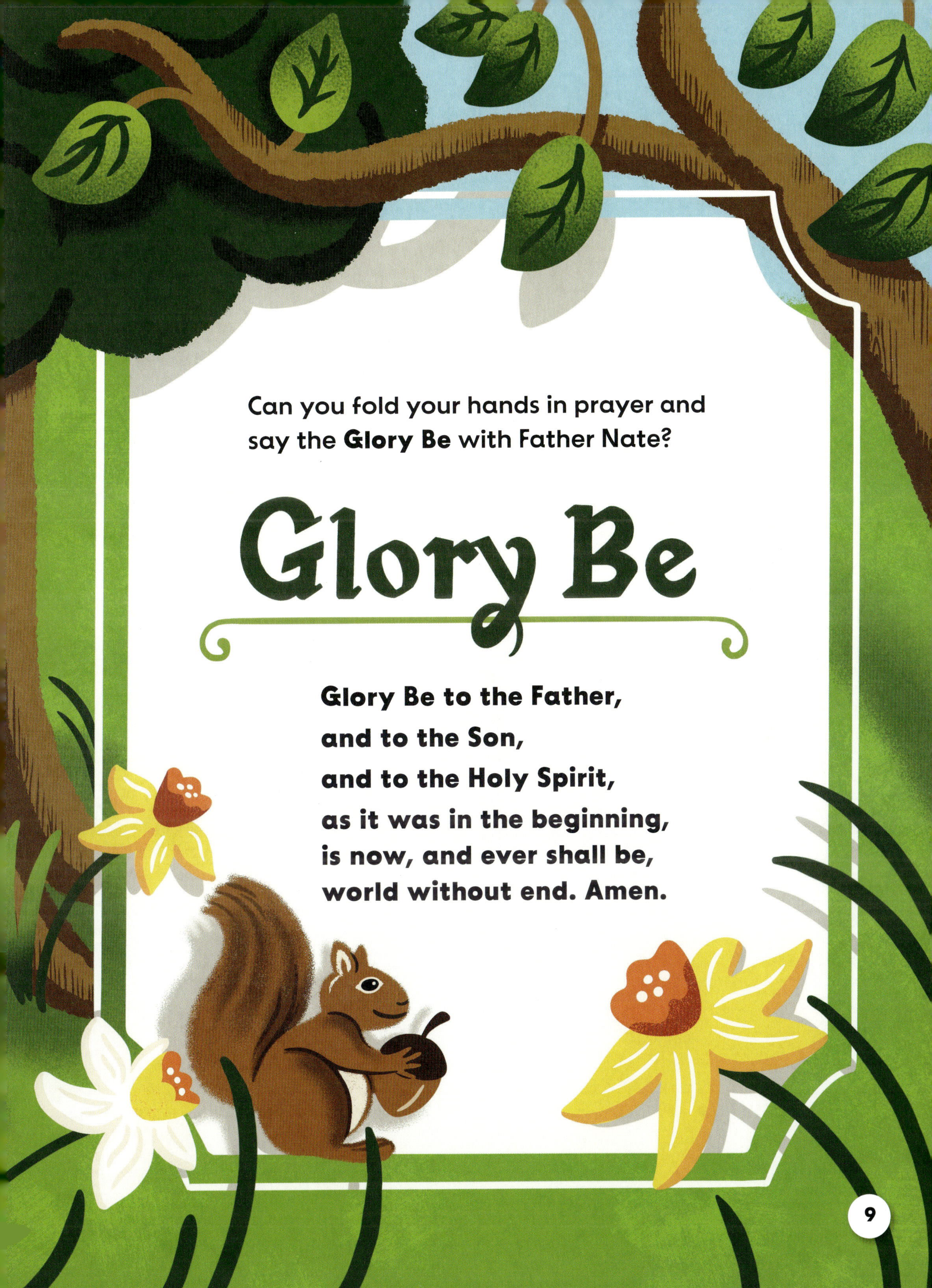

Can you fold your hands in prayer and say the **Glory Be** with Father Nate?

Glory Be

Glory Be to the Father,
and to the Son,
and to the Holy Spirit,
as it was in the beginning,
is now, and ever shall be,
world without end. Amen.

Lent is a special time of year when we ask Jesus to help us live a good life. Our Lenten Adventure lasts **40 days!** The first day is called **Ash Wednesday**. During Mass on Ash Wednesday, Father Nate places ashes on the foreheads of all the people in church. Sometimes, the ashes are placed in a cross symbol. The ashes come from burning the palms from last year's Palm Sunday. The ashes are a sign that we are sorry for our sins.

Lent is a time to ask for forgiveness.

During Lent, the Church asks us not to eat meat on Fridays. This is called **abstinence.** You can also choose to give up something, like candy or playing video games. Father Nate says to do a kind act each day of Lent. These actions help us become closer to God and remember all the good things he has done for us.

What other actions help us become closer to God?

You may have already received the sacrament of **penance**, also called **reconciliation** or **confession.** People often go to confession during Lent.

During confession, we talk to a priest about what we have done wrong since our last confession. At the end of confession, the priest will ask you to say the **Act of Contrition** prayer. Contrition means being sorry for doing something wrong.

Can you say the **Act of Contrition** prayer with Father Nate?

Act of Contrition

Oh my God, I am sorry for my sins
with all my heart.
In choosing to do wrong,
and failing to do good,
I have sinned against you
whom I love above all things.
I firmly intend, with your help,
to do penance, to sin no more,
and to avoid whatever leads me
to sin.
Our Savior Jesus Christ suffered
and died for us.
In his name, my God, have mercy.
Amen.

In Lent, there are saints whom Father Nate likes to remember. On March 17th, Father Nate celebrates St. Patrick's Day. Saint Patrick was a man who helped spread the Catholic faith to the people in Ireland. He taught people about Jesus and all of Jesus' good works.

On St. Patrick's feast day, people often celebrate by wearing green.

Another special feast day is the **Solemnity of Saint Joseph**. Joseph was the husband of Mary, the Mother of God. He helped Mary raise Jesus and was Jesus' earthly father figure. Saint Joseph was a carpenter. He was an important part of Jesus' life, and, for that reason, we celebrate and remember him on **March 19th**.

On **March 25th,** Father Nate celebrates a special feast day called the **Solemnity of the Annunciation of the Lord.** On this day, we remember when the Angel Gabriel appeared to Mary and told her she would have a baby named Jesus. The Angel Gabriel told Mary that Jesus would be God's only son. This day is special because Jesus would soon be born!

Throughout the year and during Lent, Father Nate spends time reading the Bible. One of his favorite passages is John 3:16.

Scripture Passage

"For God so loved the world that he gave his only Son, so that everyone who believes in him might not perish but might have eternal life."

During Lent, people often gather and pray the **Stations of the Cross**. Father Nate takes time to remember the steps leading up to Jesus' death.

This is both a sad and joyful time because we remember that Jesus died for all of us so our sins can be forgiven.

Stations of the Cross

Station 1: Jesus is condemned to death

Station 2: Jesus accepts the cross

Station 3: Jesus falls the first time

Station 4: Jesus meets his mother

Station 5: Simon of Cyrene helps Jesus carry his cross

Station 6: Veronica wipes the face of Jesus

Station 7: Jesus falls a second time

Station 8: Jesus meets the women of Jerusalem

Station 9: Jesus falls a third time

Station 10: Jesus is stripped of his clothes

Station 11: Jesus is crucified

Station 12: Jesus dies on the cross

Station 13: Jesus' body is taken down from the cross

Station 14: Jesus is laid in the tomb

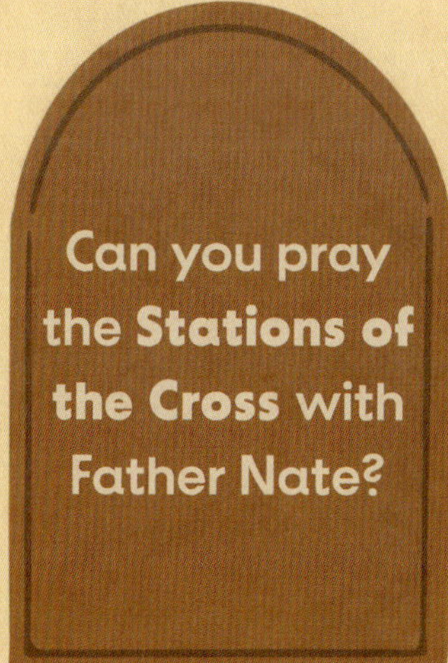

Palm Sunday is when Jesus came to Jerusalem riding on a donkey.

Father Nate explains that Jesus rode a donkey as a sign of humility. A horse was a sign of power and wealth.

Jesus entered the city in peace. A long time before Jesus was born, a prophet named Zechariah said, "Your king is coming to you... humble, and riding on a donkey" (Zechariah 9:9).

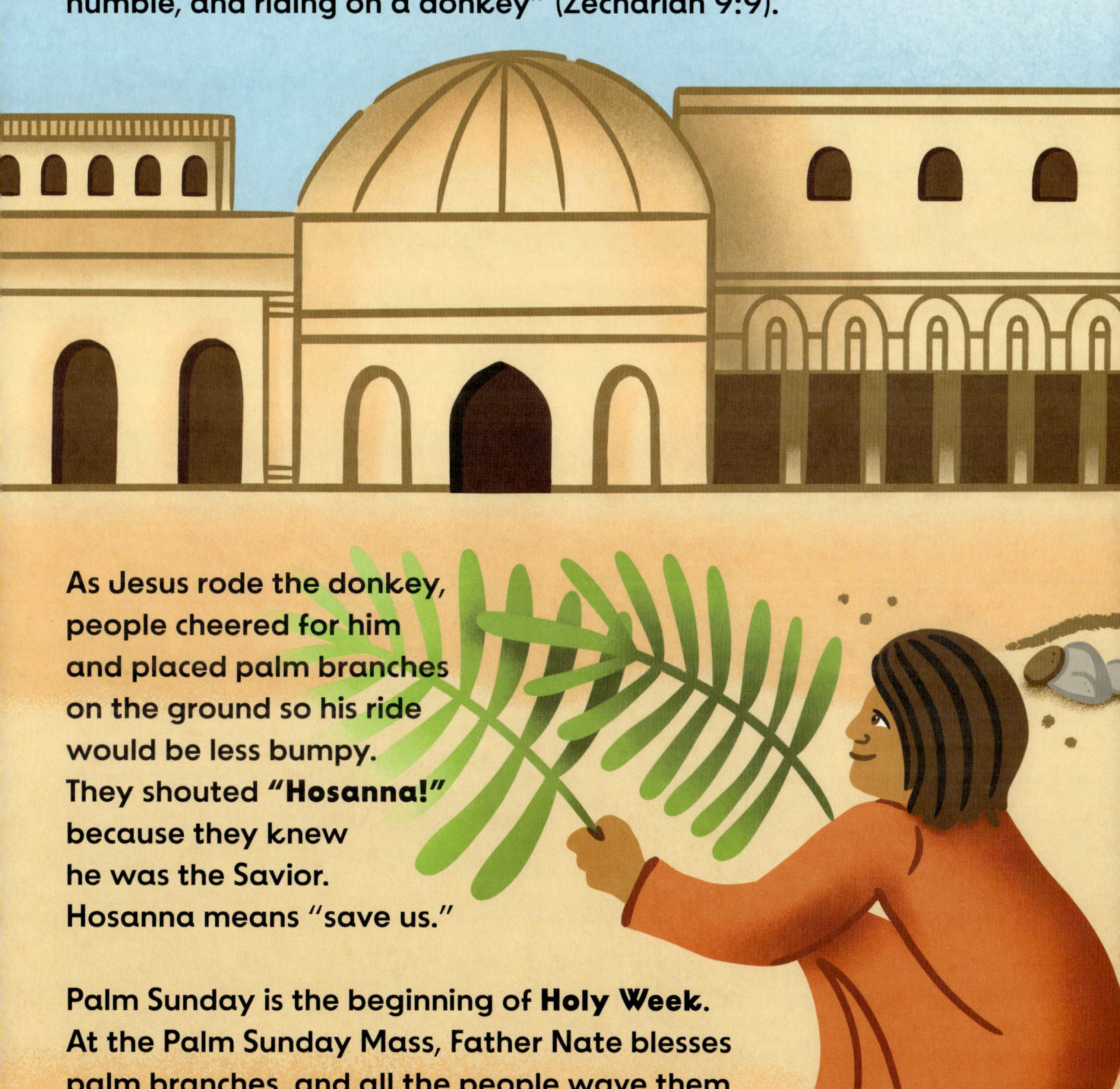

As Jesus rode the donkey, people cheered for him and placed palm branches on the ground so his ride would be less bumpy. They shouted **"Hosanna!"** because they knew he was the Savior. Hosanna means "save us."

Palm Sunday is the beginning of **Holy Week.** At the Palm Sunday Mass, Father Nate blesses palm branches, and all the people wave them and sing "Hosanna."

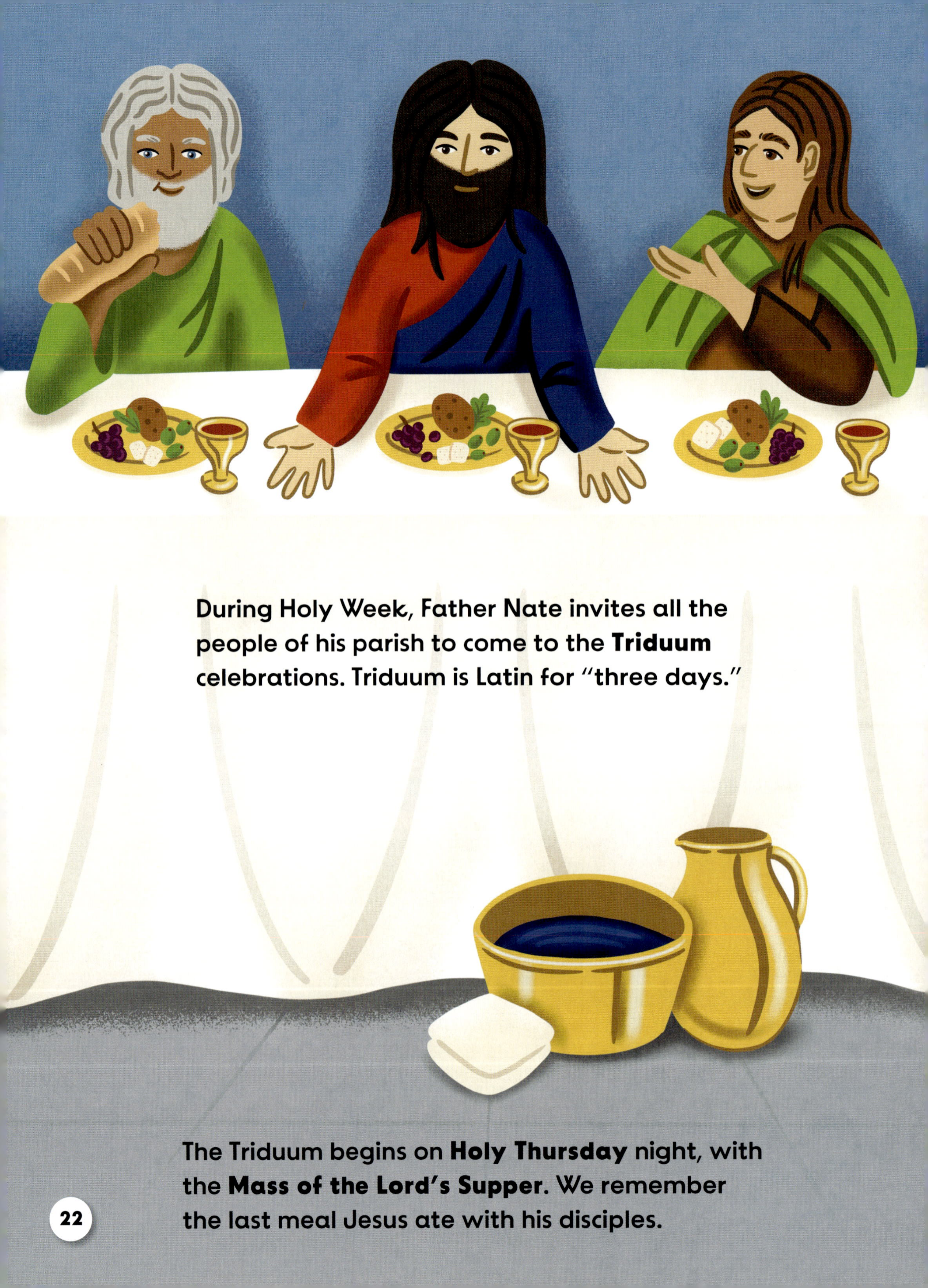

During Holy Week, Father Nate invites all the people of his parish to come to the **Triduum** celebrations. Triduum is Latin for "three days."

The Triduum begins on **Holy Thursday** night, with the **Mass of the Lord's Supper**. We remember the last meal Jesus ate with his disciples.

Before eating, **Jesus washed the feet of his twelve disciples.** During the Mass celebrated on **Holy Thursday, Father Nate washes the feet of twelve people.** This reminds us of the **love** that Jesus had for his disciples and for all of us today.

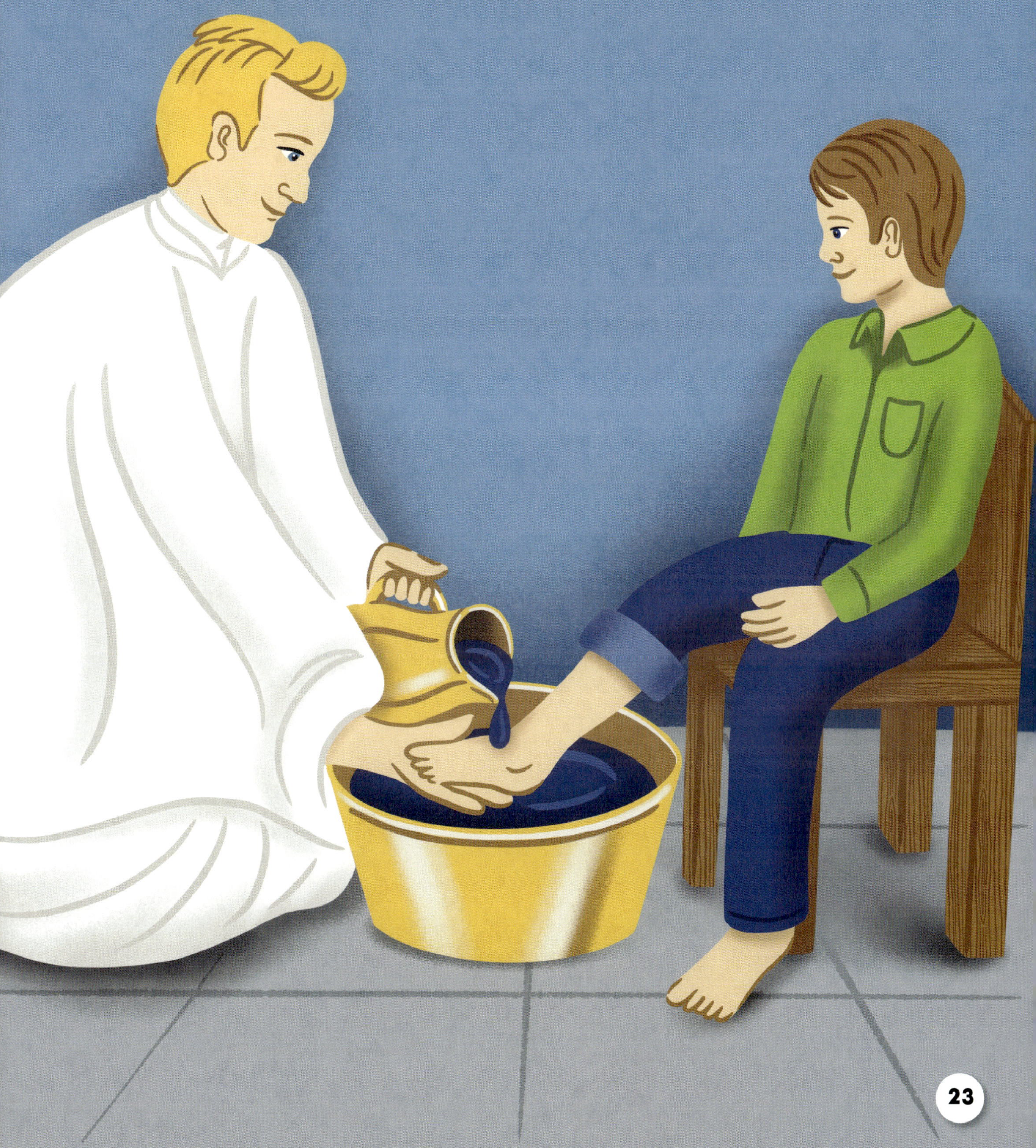

Good Friday is the second day of the Triduum. We remember **The Passion of the Lord**, when Jesus was crucified. All the people in church are invited to come forward and kiss or bow to the cross.

After Jesus died on the cross, his body was wrapped in cloths and taken to a tomb for burial.

Can you write a note to Jesus, thanking him for his sacrifice?

The third day of the Triduum begins on **Holy Saturday**. In the evening, the **Easter Vigil** is celebrated. There is a big fire, and Father Nate lights the Easter candle from the fire. Everyone in church will receive a candle. There are readings, prayers, and songs that tell our Christian story. For the first time since Lent began, Father Nate sings the Alleluia before the gospel. Will you join Father Nate in singing the Alleluia?

Father Nate continues celebrating the resurrection of Jesus on **Easter Sunday**. The church will look very special, with many flowers reminding us of new life, and the **Easter candle**, because Jesus is the Light of the World.

Father Nate explains that after Holy Saturday, some of Jesus' disciples visited the tomb where Jesus was laid to rest. But he wasn't there! His disciples realized that **God had raised Jesus from the dead!**

This is a time of great joy because Jesus has forgiven our sins, and we will live forever with God.

Father Nate says, "We owe everything to God, so please spend time with him every day. Say your prayers, be kind to others, and thank God every day for the gifts of forgiveness and everlasting life."

Jesus rose on Easter dawn;
The stone by his tomb was rolled away.
He conquered death on that morn,
To live forever and show us the way.

Lord Jesus,
thank you for showing us the way,
for teaching us how to live,
and for dying and rising for us.
Help us remember your love for us,
so that we can be better at loving others. Amen.

What is one thing you will do this week to...

...show your love for your family?

...show your love for your friends?

...show your love for Jesus?

About the Authors & Illustrator

Mia Toschi is a four-time Emmy Award–winning television news reporter from New York City who has shared stories about faith from all over the world. Mia has an MA in education and is a parishioner and volunteer at her local parish. This is her fourth book and third children's book.

Madalyn Allender is the director of religious education and director of parish operations for her home parish in Indiana. She is also a former teacher in both elementary and special education. Her passion is guiding children through their faith journey and helping form them as disciples.

Amanda Jozaitis is a designer and illustrator in Indiana. Known for her vibrant, playful, contemporary style, she incorporates intricate details, textures, and hand lettering inspired by vintage design.